To OUR GOO[D]
NEIGHBOUR!

AWNE

Doug & Dawn

THINK HEADLINES

Turning *your* stories into headlines

Douglas C. Woods

WESTBOW
PRESS®
A DIVISION OF THOMAS NELSON
& ZONDERVAN

WestBow Press books may be ordered through booksellers or by contacting:

WestBow Press
A Division of Thomas Nelson & Zondervan
1663 Liberty Drive
Bloomington, IN 47403
www.westbowpress.com
844-714-3454

Editing by Glenn G. Woods, Cover concept by Enoch Tee

ISBN: 978-1-6642-3282-2 (sc)
ISBN: 978-1-6642-3283-9 (e)

Library of Congress Control Number: 2021915055

Print information available on the last page.

WestBow Press rev. date: 7/23/2021

CONTENTS

Dedicated to the memory of my father, Rev. Robert F. Woods, the best promoter I have ever known. He dedicated his entire life promoting the best news ever broadcast.

FOREWORD

The writer of Ecclesiastes ......"Of making many books there is no end, and much study wearies the body". Ecclesiastes 12:12 NIV.

So, do we really need another book? Do we really need more information? That depends on what you are looking for. "THINK HEADLINES" might appear, at first glance, to be self-serving. Might we also use a title like "Attention Getter" or "Look at us". One could be forgiven if that is one's first reaction. But I urge you to go a little further, pressing on to understand the value of becoming aware not so much of the purveyors of ministry, but the reason for ministry.

The writer brings us into the picture, almost as if we all were there. You can almost smell the Christmas Dinner being prepared at the mission (either in Winnipeg or Vancouver). The scenes are indeed word pictures that tell the story of life for so many.

The reason we need another book, and one like this is, is due to the fact that we all have a story, and yet not all get to tell it. Surely one of the reasons that "not for profit" organizations exist, is to assist government in making life work. Getting these stories into the media network provides clear evidence that we are doing what we were called to do. Clergy and laypeople alike become the conduit and flow of information to a world that perhaps wonders what it is we actually do.

The "Principles", accompanied by real life stories are portable. So often we can become discouraged because what works in one place just won't work where we are. But this is different. The context of ministry might be different, but the portability afforded in these principles is so very encouraging.

Sure, not all publicity is easy to deal with, and yes, some publicity will thwart the forward movement of any mission, but just for a while.

In "THINK HEADLINES" Doug Woods has captured for us, in conversational script, the essence of using an existing vehicle, that in many cases is looking for opportunities to tell community stories, and, we all have one to tell!

So yes, "Of making many books there is no end, and much study wearies the body", but make room for this one.

Dr. Ian Fitzpatrick
National Director Church of the Nazarene Canada

PREFACE

One of the surprises of my life was making the headlines. I never dreamt it would happen. In fact I never thought that any initiative of mine would ever result in making headlines. This book is about how it happened and the practices that I learned to make it happen repeatedly. These insights have the potential to propel your organization into headlines. Publicity is foundational to organizations, especially those that operate on a shoe string. You can be a top story simply by following these principles and easy to understand practices that I will outline. This book contains the stories behind the headlines. I write with both the personal experience and the persuasion that regardless of how small your organization is it can be a featured story that hits the headlines. The establishment of good media relations requires insight, preparation, and media savvy. I will provide all these elements for you. These chapters will inform you both how it happened in my tenure as an executive director of two Canadian compassionate non-profit organizations, and how it can also be your experience. If you follow these principles you can become proficient in capturing public attention time and time again. By following this prescribed formula you will get that media coverage that you need and no one will send you an invoice.

By reading these chapter you will learn:

- How to tell your story to the media with minimal cost.
- How you can position your organization to make the headlines.
- How to communicate your story in the various media as simple as A B C.
- How to identify your best media prospects.
- How to market your event/product

You'll come away with:

- A game plan for reaching out to the media
- An action plan for telling your story.
- Ways to sell your story to the media in ways they can't resist.
- Expertise in generating publicity for your organization.

In the fall of 1998 as the executive director of Siloam Mission I was invited by the City of Winnipeg to sell our building at 707 Main Street. This building was only about thirty feet wide, had a dugout basement and was three stories high, though the top two were unsuitable for any foreseeable future development. The city was in the early stages of developing a comprehensive plan to change the face of the inner city neighbourhood in the North end of Winnipeg. This was all in preparation for the coming 1999 PAN AM Games. The group heading up this development project was called the North Main Task Force. It was co-chaired by Joe Bova and Mary Richard. Their initial offer of $ 75,000 to Siloam Mission was according to our research a fair market value offer, but it was inadequate to allow this vital street ministry to continue. I say vital because we were helping connect the marginalized people of North Main Street with the middle class people of Winnipeg. The eventual settlement of this proposed transaction would be at a level far beyond that initial fair market offer. The reason for this successful conclusion was for the most part due to the media helping us tell our story.

Siloam Mission has become a significant compassionate organization in the City of Winnipeg serving the homeless and the working poor. However, at the time when the City made that initial offer the Mission had been operating out of this old three story building for over thirteen years. This building which was located

SILOAM MISSION BECAME A NATIONAL HEADLINE.

near the former CPR railway station had once been the site of Alexander's Café. The Mission had been serving annually about thirteen thousands meals. Four times a week Siloam would open its doors to all sorts of street people. In addition to serving meals it had been providing weekly free clothing and toiletries to more than two hundred and fifty families in the immediate neighbourhood. The significant factor was not just the numbers of meals that were being served, but how these meals and clothing items were served. As Rev. Rick Burk, a former executive director, often said, Siloam Mission was a "welcoming place" for people that other social agencies in the area would often turn away. It had become a place of refuge for the "sniffers", for the prostitutes, and numerous other social outcasts. Because of these core values its leadership had no intention of disrupting this practice of serving these marginalized people of the North Main Street, the people that few others really cared about.

Gavin Wood, the Mission's lawyer at that time helped guide Siloam through those protracted discussions with the City. He helped draft and articulate what became a winning strategy. He saw to it that throughout this period of intensive negotiations with city officials that the Mission leadership contention that it was providing valued service to a very needy

THE SECOND POOREST POSTAL CODE IN ALL OF CANADA.

neighbourhood was heard. The board communicated their intention to continue providing these essential services to an impoverished segment of the city's population. Further, Mr. Wood pointed out that if the Mission were to accept the city's initial fair market offer it would have made it financially impossible to reposition Siloam Mission in a new location in a neighbourhood that was considered the second poorest postal code in all of Canada.

As this negotiation process dragged on between the City and Siloam Mission it became increasingly a frequent news conversation. Siloam Mission had been in the papers before because of its social care. For example earlier in the year Marc Piche, a correspondent of the community paper The Metro, had written a story about Mrs. Louise White. "Granny White" as she was affectionately known had for eleven years prepared meals for street people because she had a heart for the working poor and the hungry on North Main Street. Rick Burk, a former executive director had observed her cooking skills and commented that *"Mrs. White had an amazing heart and the ability to turn the incredible diverse food donations into hearty meals."*

STARTED THE WAVE

First it was CBC Radio's reporter David White who did a story in the midst of these negotiations. He reported about the Mission's compassionate and loving service to those of the inner city for more than a decade. In his report he included sound bites of the music played the night he was there. His report was broadcast on CBC Radio's "Information Morning Show" a couple of days later. After David had interviewed me that night he cornered me and asked what was the city offering? I said to him, as I would tell other reporters in the weeks to come that I thought it was not wise to disclose the amounts being discussed. He respected my response and dropped the subject.

A couple days later The Winnipeg Sun published a report that essentially opened up the flood gates of media attention. Reporter Sherry Kubara had phoned me at home on a Sunday afternoon. After her telephone interview she asked if they could take some pictures of the Mission to include in her report. I agreed and so later that day I met one of the Sun's staff photographers at the Mission.

The article appeared the following morning on January 11th. The report was accompanied with a full colour photograph of me sitting in the empty Mission. In her article headlined, "Native

NATIVE CENTRE HELD "HOSTAGE"

Centre held hostage", she cited that city officials blamed the Mission for holding the Neeginan Healing Centre project hostage. The Mission site had become one of the key sites of this development. I found this article disappointing at the time because of some its errors. As my son Stephen teased me, "I bristled". For example among the article's errors it had stated that I was the owner of Siloam Mission. More than that the article had essentially positioned the Mission in a bad light, a posture that did not reflect the reality of Siloam's track record of providing valued service to a very impoverished neighbourhood. However, in reflection I am thankful for the Sun's article because it opened the media flood gates and started a wave with numerous requests for interviews from various other local media outlets.

The same day that the Sun published their article I was interviewed on radio station CJOB, Manitoba's largest radio station, 1290 AM Talk Radio, and CBC-TV's John Webb. John Webb was among the first. When he asked me for an interview I expressed some hesitation. I cited the inaccurate reporting of The Winnipeg Sun. He appreciated my viewpoint, but persuaded me that he would provide a more balanced report. That afternoon he interviewed me at Siloam Mission. True to his word his report that was aired later that evening was both balanced and fair.

That Monday, which was filled with a series of lows and highs taught me the reality that the media frequently feeds off one another. I experienced firsthand that if one news outlet publishes a good story it is certain the rest of the media you will take note and would likely followed it up with another newsworthy angle.

The news coverage eventually slowed down to a trickle. Then about a week later came the news break that changed the entire tone of the negotiations. Jonathan Gravenor a correspondent of CTV National News contacted me. He inquired if he could do a story about the Mission and the negotiations with the City. He remarked that he had been watching this story as it had been developing over the past couple of weeks. He commented that he had observed that often there was a lack of appreciation by city officials elsewhere for Christian missions in urban areas. I agreed to an interview with the usual stipulation that his cameraman respect those guests of the Mission that might not wish to be seen on television for various reasons. The story aired nationally on the last Saturday of that month. Its tone was very sympathetic. It gave some background on how the Mission had served the neighbourhood for the past thirteen years. One media consultant informed me afterwards that those three minutes of air time time on national TV was equivalent to $ 150,000 in advertising value. That report proved to be the turning point in the Mission's saga.

That evening after the cameras were turned off Gravenor asked me what the city was offering. I felt prompted for the first time to disclose the actual amount the city was offering. I told him seventy-five thousand dollars. The night our story was aired it went coast to coast. In that headline item I was able to tell our story that, *"The mission needed much more money to start over."* I argued that. Gravenor commented that *"The city is pinching pennies with people who depend on pennies to survive."* That did it!

"THE CITY IS PINCHING PENNIES WITH PEOPLE WHO DEPEND ON PENNIES TO SURVIVE."

Ten days later after that CTV National report aired the city brought us a brand new offer of $ 150, 000, double of that of the original offer. Further negotiations resulted in a quick settlement of $ 165,000 plus legal, storage, and moving costs. By early March the City of Winnipeg had taken possession of the 707 Main Street property. Ten days later the Winnipeg Free Press was reporting that demolition work was well underway with a picture of the walls of the former Alexandra Café building being demolished.

FREE PRESS
MARCH 11/89

KEN GIGLIOTTI/WINNIPEG FREE PRESS

Tumbling down

The Siloam Mission building at 707 Main St. is torn down yesterday to make way for the $12-million Neeginan aboriginal roundhouse and park at Main Street and Higgins Avenue.

I believe that it was the cumulative effect of those numerous media reports that helped us tell our story in such a convincing way that eventually led to this acceptable settlement. This fair and just agreement enabled Siloam Mission to relocate less than a year later further south at 564 Main Street just a block from Winnipeg's City Hall. Three decades later Siloam Mission not only continues to provide valued service, but serves with far greater and expanded and expanded services to the homeless and the working poor. All this because we were able to inform the public about the humanitarian work of Siloam Mission through the media in its various platforms.

If your organization is doing good work in your city people should know about it. If your society is providing valued service in your community as is Siloam Mission then let the neighbourhood know. If what you are doing is meeting needs, and changing lives, then why not let others know about it. This is what publicity is. Telling the world your story.

PUBLICITY IS LETTING
THE WORLD KNOW

Marketing is essential to every organization. Whether it is a business, a political party, or a non-profit group its existence depends upon effectively communicating its message, telling its story, informing buyers about their products, communicating to the electorate what it's platform is. The form such marketing takes may be a multiplatform advertising plan or simply by informal word of mouth. The truth is that without some form of intentional communication even the best of organizations will likely falter.

The fact that good marketing is essential to every organization is especially so for non-profit groups. Each organization needs what it is doing circulated in order to sustain financial support and to recruit enthusiastic volunteers. People need to know about their good works and how their activity is enriching community life. Without sustained good publicity even the best institution will suffer eventual decline. Foundational to fundraising and the recruitment of volunteers is good PR. This is an essential ingredient. How an organization is perceived is of strategic importance to its sustainability

CAN BE ACHIEVED AT
A MINIMAL COST

One of the constant challenges that faces especially smaller non-profit organizations is the cost of communication. How can your story be told beyond the perimeters of your organization with the limited funds at your disposal? A prevalent way for small community groups to communicate their cause is through a newsletter. Usually this newsletter is circulated either by hand or direct mail. However to be more effective other methods need to be incorporated in a broader communication plan. Effective communication strategies need to include other media. For example a retail store will employ as a part of their promotion plan a wider communication package which includes newspapers, radio, and TV advertisements. This insures that the intended target audience is effectively informed about its merchandise. Small non-profit groups cannot usually at first afford to budget such an advertising campaign. It can be too great a financial risk.

There is an option for smaller groups to communicate their activities and good causes to the public. The good news is this can be achieved at a smaller financial investment. It will take time, but your group can capture the public's attention and tell your story to those who are potential supporters of your cause. By implementing these simple principles your group even though small in size can tell it's story and can tell it effectively.

This book is written with grass roots, non-profit organizations who need to tell their story in mind. The principles however will apply to any size association or society that has a cause that needs to be told. Whether your group was organized yesterday or ten years ago these principles will work.

THE PRINCIPLES
THAT WORK

I have been using these theories of communication successfully for more than thirty years, first as a pastor of churches in small rural communities, then most recently as an executive director of two inner city missions in two of Canada's largest cities. It was events in Winnipeg as executive director of Siloam Mission that initially helped me identify these principles. Since then they have worked for me repeatedly. So I know they will work for you too! You do not need a degree in journalism or communication. Just continue to read this book and apply these four principles to your current situation. Then you can begin reaping the benefits of telling your story in tomorrow's newspaper. You can turn your story into headlines!

- The media can increase the public's awareness of your group
- The media can help recruit members to your group
- The media can inform the community of what you are doing and what you have done
- The media can raise public awareness about various issues

To persuade you that these principles will actually work for you and your group I will illustrate them with real life examples. Some of these stories were about my work, for example how our Christmas Dinner was featured as headline on the front page of the Winnipeg largest newspaper. Another is about how a friend's hobby made the headlines not once, but twice. These headline stories occurred not just in community newspapers, but also on local television. It can happen in your situation. In fact it will happen if you incorporate these principles and practices. Use these four media principles as stepping stones in making your organization better known.

ONE

THE NEWS MEDIA ARE A BUSINESS

Principle One: The first principle is understanding that essentially the news media is a business which gathers and disseminates information. They generate income first by collecting information and then broadcasting that information to their respective audiences. That is their business. Understanding this first principle is fundamental to helping organizations in telling their story. As commercial banks require deposits so does the media. Both need regular streams of deposits if they are to operate successfully. The difference is in the nature of the deposits. To a commercial bank they need monetary deposits before they can offer loans and mortgages. To the media the deposit is news about an event that has happened or is about to happen. Information is their commodity. Information to the media is as valuable as money is to a financial institution. .

Take for example a daily newspaper. Imagine as they were preparing for tomorrow's edition the newsroom could not find any leads of potential stories. The editors scratched their heads for some ideas. They called the major's office and different city councillors about the issues that might be on the next week's city council's agenda. No one returned their calls. They send reporters to the police headquarters to inquire about any recent arrests. The fire chief offers no reports on recent fires and related investigations. No pictures! No stories! The chamber of commerce has no news about potential land developments or reports on business trends. Even the professional and community sports teams offered no potential stories on trades or game scores. It would appear in such a scenario that nothing was happening in the local community. But imagine if this scenario did occur. Tomorrow's newspaper would have no headlines. The sports reporters would have nothing to write in their columns. The pages would be blank except for advertisements. On the radio at the top of the hour the announcer would have to confess there was nothing to report. No breaking news. Of course things were happening. Every day in every community and every part of the nation there are newsworthy events. The business of the media in every part of the world and in your community where things are happening is to report them. The media need continual news feeds about world events and what is happening locally in your neighbourhood. It may be from political world, from the entertainment world, from the sports scene or from organizations like yours that things are happening. The media in all its forms and branches need information. Without such deposits the newspapers, the radio and the television have nothing to publish or broadcast. So why not make a news deposit?

Your organization whether it is a large corporation like General Motors or a small mom and pop corner store represent potential sources of information that some sector of the media will be interested in hearing about. In order to gather such stories some radio outlets have offered to their listeners $ 25.00 of free air time on their cell phone for the best news tip of the week. The reason for these incentives is they need that information and in some instances are prepared to pay for it. Radio stations view those in their listening audience as potential sources of information. They need traffic reports, weather reports, and sports reports.

Recognize that your organization possesses a commodity which is of value to local newspapers and radio stations. The media needs you! So if you know of such information why not make a deposit?

NEWSPAPERS NEED CONTINUAL NEWS FEED

Tell the media about an event that may be of potential interest to their readers and viewers. I suspect that a significant number of the stories that are broadcast are placed in the media hands by someone just like you. The rest of stories aired are the result of research by that particular media. So why not tell them your story? Put in their hands the information they need. There are reporters who are receptive to the news that you know about. They need your news tip. They welcome captivating news releases. Give the media useful leads and information. Give them what they need…news!

CHAPTER SUMMARY

- The media is in the business of gathering and distributing information.
- Their commodity is news.
- The media constantly needs new sources of information.

Your organization is a potential news source.

TWO

KNOW YOUR MEDIA

Principle Two: Every news media outlet is different in some aspect. So it is important that you understand the significances of these distinctions as you work with them. Start by familiarizing yourself with the media that speaks to your demographic and geographic circumstances. Do the research. For example recognize there are differences in the sizes of media outlets. Some are weeklies, dailies, student papers, cable news, and others are the big players, local and national TV stations. Start a file with the contact information of these respective outlets. Use this list to make periodic phone calls with these reporters and editors. Check out the web their sites.

For example the Canadian Broadcasting Corporation is one of the largest news agencies in Canada. It has enormous resources in reporters alone compared to such small media outlets as the Shelburne Ontario Free Press and Economist. While this community newspaper publishes only once a week the CBC broadcasts daily in both official Canadian languages on both radio and television. CBC-TV and CTV focus through their local affiliates on both local and national news stories. Another contrast is the medium which a news outlet employs. One is print and the other is electronic. Knowledge of these differences is another factor in telling your organization's story.

EVERY MEDIA OUTLET
IS DIFFERENT

When I was serving as the executive director of Mission Possible in Vancouver we tapped into several different media. For example when Dawn and I first moved from Winnipeg to the Vancouver area I sent a news release to one of the local community newspapers that covered the Tri-Cities of the Vancouver suburban municipalities. The timeline and nature of the news are factors in news coverage. I recognized that this media would probably be more receptive to covering our arrival in that area than one of the larger dailies like the Vancouver Sun or the Province. The key factor was the coverage area. The other newspapers covered the greater Vancouver area while the Tri-City News focused on things happening in the Coquitlam and the Port Coquitlam area. The result was first a telephone interview. Than later in the week a photographer came and took a picture of Dawn, myself, and Rev. Gordon McCann, a local pastor who supported the ministry of Mission Possible.

Another example was the arrival at Mission Possible of a Youth for Christ group from Lacombe, Alberta. Their task was to paint the interior of our building on Powell Street. While in the Downtown Eastside they would have opportunities to observe aspects of a Canadian skid row. I had made contact earlier with a reporter from a community newspaper called The Vancouver Courier. This paper's focus was the Vancouver scene. So I sent a news release to various media outlets, but the target of this particular NR was the Vancouver Courier. The result was an interview by Kevin Kinghorn and his article on this Alberta work and witness team. The headline of his article was *"Christian teens from Alberta see gritty Downtown Eastside"*. It was such a good story that we put a link to it on our web site. Kevin wrote about these vibrant young people from a rural community in central Alberta. He told about the contrast of life in their small farming town and the poverty of Vancouver's Downtown Eastside as seen through their eyes.

"CHRISTIAN TEENS FROM ALBERTA SEE GRITTY DOWNTOWN EASTSIDE"

This provided excellent publicity about Mission Possible and the Youth for Christ group that put this trip together.

In December 2001 we sent out information detailing our plans to have our guests at the Mission Possible Christmas Dinner raise funds for Afghanistan. We announced that we had distributed free tickets to 210 people inviting them to be our guests at our fabulous Christmas Dinner. The difference was that we were inviting each guest from Vancouver's Downtown Eastside to bring a loonie (Canadian dollar) to donate to the people of Afghanistan through the auspices of the Canadian Foodgrains Bank. Our goal was to raise $ 200 which would be matched by Canadian International Development Agency through CFGB at a ratio of four dollars to every dollar donated. The release went out to a number of local media, but the prime target of this news release was BC CTV. I knew there would be some interest by them since they had already covered other stories about Mission Possible. On the Saturday evening of our Christmas Dinner they aired a two minute story about the poor giving to others in need on their early edition and then later on their eleven o'clock broadcast.

Some stories are not fit for print, but are more suited for visual effect. This was a story that had to be seen. So research the media that you are endeavoring to tell your story through. Read, listen, watch and even call them asking them what kind of stories they are looking for. You can help yourself by helping the media tell your story.

SOME STOIRES ARE NOT FIT FOR PRINT

Knowledge of each respective media includes also an understanding of the market they are targeting. That market will determine the nature of the news they are interested in gathering. A national television outlet will be looking for stories of interest to the entire country. That story may be local, but if it is large enough it could capture headlines coast to coast.

Some stories will not generate any interest beyond the immediate area. For example I had the opportunity to officiate at the wedding of a lovely young couple while I was the pastor of the Elmwood Church of the Nazarene in Winnipeg. During my preliminary conversations with Dave and Esther a couple of days before their wedding I learned of their plans that immediately after the wedding ceremony they were going to a neighbourhood ice cream parlor called Sub Zero. During their courtship they would often stop there during the hot weather and enjoy the delicious dairy products. It was a well-known place that Dawn and I had also frequented. I recognized that this was a potential news story. It would not fit the national scene, but it would be a human interest story perhaps for a small community newspaper. So with Dave and Esther's permission I phoned the local community paper, The Herald. The Herald is one of those papers with plenty of advertisements and community stories that is delivered free to every household in the neighbourhood. I informed them of Dave and Esther's plans. The Herald sent a free-lance photographer who took a beautiful picture of Esther and Dave in their formal wedding attire on the front steps of Sub Zero. Next week on the front page in full colour was the picture of Dave holding an ice cream cone for his bride.

There were some perks for making that arrangement. There was first the satisfaction of successfully making this arrangement. I knew that this picture would probably find its way eventually into the wedding scrapbook of Dave and Esther. For Nina, the proprietor of Sub Zero some good will, and exposure for her thriving business. This also helped me cultivate a relationship with Wanda McConnell the editor of The Herald that paved the way for future stories. It was a big win for everyone, a young couple, a small neighbourhood business, a local newspaper. And an ice cream treat for Dawn and myself.

So if you want to crack the media barrier in your neighbourhood read their paper, listen to their top of the hour broadcasts and watch their news coverage.

CHAPTER SUMMARY

- Recognize the differences between media.
- Research the market they serve.
- Note the nature of news they feature.

THREE

MAKE FRIENDS WITH THE MEDIA

Principle Three: Without question media exposure is the most powerful way to gain attention, credibility, and clout. The news media have been described as the modern gate keepers. They like the gate keepers of ancient walled cities determine who comes in and who goes out. These contemporary gate keepers possess enormous power concerning what the public views and reads. There is no doubt in my thinking that media exposure is the most powerful way to gain attention. Whether it is an interview with a newspaper reporter or being featured as an expert on radio or television the potential impact and promotional potential are unlimited. So make it one of your goals is to make friends with the media. This will help to put your organization on the map.

I have witnessed events that were reported quite differently from what I saw. Clayton Young formerly of 1290 Talk Radio in Winnipeg told me in an interview that the media does at times have their own agenda in reporting events. Their agenda will intentionally colour the news stories they air. In this twenty-first century TV stations, journalist, editors, reporters, publishers, may seem to be daunting but good working relationships with them can happen. The bottom line is the media whether on screen or the printed page is a powerful influence and you can tap into it.

MAKE FRIENDS WITH THE MEDIA

These factors alone should inspire you to follow this third principle in dealing with the media. The individuals who work in the editorial rooms of newspapers and television are people. They are people who respond in positive ways when treated with respect just as we do. So it is important if you wish to tell your story about the work you are doing to build bridges to those who do the reporting and editing. So cultivate the media that is serving the area you are interested in informing. Build and maintain good relationships by mutual trust.

Develop a media information file. Make it a practice of adding details about media contacts such as names, positions, emails and fax numbers. Jot down this information and place them in your media file. Then add these details to your master media database. Cultivate your relationship.

Here are some ways to cultivate relationships in the media. For example remember principle one that this media business is exactly that, a business. So help them do their job. Make their job easy. Provide them newsworthy leads and information. In fact put these leads right in their laps. Help them with their research. As you prepare to send news releases imagine you are writing the story and ask yourself what kind of information would you need? Most media personnel do not have the resources to know what is happening in all the sectors of a community. They love to have people walk in the door with news ideas. This kind of soft news gives a balance to their overall reporting.

MAKE THEIR JOB EASY

Roger Hannon was the editor of a small weekly newspaper in Shelburne, Ontario where we were living and working at the time.

He was not only editor, but for the most part the only full time reporter of the weekly paper. I decided that I would cultivate this relationship. As a result of my relationship with Roger he featured dozens of articles about our church.

For example there was a story and picture about the clock tower of our church being painted that required a special crane to reach the top of this four story structure. Another story was about the sketch of the church by a local artist. The church facility we were using at that time had once been the local post office, with the post master living in the upstairs apartment. Another time Roger featured a college choir concert that our church was hosting at the local high school. When the youth group had a car wash to raise funds to attend a youth conference they featured a short story and picture. In addition to the news stories he covered for us I began to write a weekly column for his paper called *Life Lines*.

A NEW LOOK FOR CHURCH
The Grace Church of the Nazarene clock tower, on Owen Sound Street, under-went a new paint job on Saturday. George Flanagan and Gary Hughes were contracted to the the job one month ago.

The major benefit was the paper's coverage of our summer concerts. Our church during the summer months sponsored a well-attended event which was called Good News Concerts. The plan was that we would invite a couple of musical groups to perform on Sunday evening at the local IGA shopping plaza. They would sing and play from a temporary stage that was actually a farm wagon. It was an exciting event that allowed people from this small town of three thousand to hear inspirational music. The option was that people could either sit in their cars or on the seats we provided near the mobile stage.

Each Monday morning I would rush over to Roger's office just in time to meet the paper's weekly deadline. I would give him a news release about what happened the night before. The news releases would contain information about the musicians who had performed the night before and an announcement about those who were to perform the next Sunday evening. I made it easy for him to cover a local event without getting out of his office. One morning in our conversation I told him that I had pictures of the Good News Concerts that would fit well with the news release. But I could not find a place to have them processed in time to reach the paper's Monday deadline. Upon hearing this he got up from his desk and motioned me to follow him out to the back into the paper's darkroom. He proceeded to give me a roll of film. He then instructed me to have the film back the following Monday morning. So each Wednesday there would be a story about the concert accompanied by a photo. I was helping him do his job by reporting on a community event and he was helping us tell our story.

CANADA'S BALLADEER — Wiz Bryant performed at the first Good News Concert at the Shelburne IGA Sunday.

Bryant featured Sunday

The first Good News Concert at the Shelburne Plaza took place Sunday night featuring a local resident Mr. Wiz Bryant. Wiz who is known as Canada's balladeer

because of his T.V. appearances, captured the hearts of the audience with numerous songs including one of his most recent compositions "Man on Fire". In addition those who gathered in the local shopping plaza in their cars heard the Al Smith Trio from Alliston. The group included Al Smith's daughter Leanne and son

Saturday from Nathan Phillip's Square in Toronto where he participated in another open air concert at the Peace Garden.

Next Sunday at 7:00 p.m. the second of the series of four concerts will feature trumpeter Stan Ellidson from Collingwood, who played for Pope John. H last fall also Bee and Ev

Main St., Shelburne 925-2340

HELP THEM DO TO THEIR JOB

I built on this relationships giving him news tips about what I knew was happening around town. For example one afternoon I was in my office when I heard a fire truck come down the street. I rushed outside and saw there was a fire in the next block. I went back into the church office and phoned my editor friend Roger and gave him the news tip. This was part a of relationship that was advantageous to us both. I helped him with information for his newspaper and he helped me tell our story.

Douglas Martindale was the MLA for the Burrows Manitoba provincial riding in the north end of Winnipeg. At the time he was the New Democratic Party's opposition critic for family services in the provincial legislature. He told me in the fall of 1998 that as a project he was going to attempt to live on constraints of a welfare recipient for the entire month of September. He thought this would give him some needed perspective on this issue. So he set out to do it. He first moved a small bed into his Selkirk Avenue office along with a microwave oven. He soon found out that it was indeed a challenge. He discovered that transportation by city transit was just too costly. So he resurrected an old bicycle as his primary mode of transportation. But when it broke down he was faced with a $ 40 repair bill that shot his food budget. So he began making a habit of coming to Siloam Mission on Thursday evenings to volunteer. That was the night we put out vegetables that we could not use or had a surplus of. I admired Doug for what he was doing. I thought that this was a potential story that perhaps David White of CBC Radio might be interested in. So I passed on this news tip to Dave.

The next Thursday night while Doug was volunteering at Siloam Mission he informed me he was to be interviewed the following morning on CBC Radio about his project. I jokingly told him not to forget Siloam Mission. He didn't forget. Right at the top of the interview with CBC's morning man Terry MacLeod he spoke words of warm appreciation for the Church of the Nazarene and its ministry through Siloam Mission to the street people of Winnipeg.

Through this tip I was cultivating a relationship with a reporter who would prove to be a supporter of Siloam Mission. In fact that Christmas Dave and his wife came down to Siloam and helped serve at our Annual Christmas Dinner.

Knowing this principle prompted me to pass on another successful tip. I remember receiving in the mail a copy of the University of Winnipeg Alumni paper, The Journal. As I read it I noticed there were a number of stories about graduates and what they were doing since their graduation. I knew that my predecessor at Siloam Mission was a graduate of the University as I was. Rick Burk was at that time a chaplain for a federal penitentiary in Saskatchewan. I also knew that Rick was coming back to Winnipeg to do a workshop the following weekend. So I sent the editor of The Journal a news release about how both of us were grads of the university and were both connected with the Siloam Mission.

The end result was a story in the spring issue of the Journal about both of us entitled *"Agents of Grace"*. It was a two page story with full colour photos about how our ministry at Siloam Mission had impacted our personal lives. The story of our ministry to the street people of Winnipeg in that context had a narrow appeal, but it proved to be newsworthy to associate Editor Paula Denbow. To her it was about two graduates from their faculty of Theology who were making a difference serving the marginalized people of our society on Winnipeg's North Main Street strip.

Speaking of Rick Burk, I connected him with reporter Glen MacKenzie of the Winnipeg Free Press five years earlier. Rick had gone to speak at a youth conference in Edmonton Alberta in May 1995. He had challenged the teens at that conference that if they raised $ 3,000 for Siloam Mission he'd let them cut his hair. The young people surprised him and raised $ 4,000. He returned to Winnipeg with little hair. To me that was a story. Glen MacKenzie of the Free Press thought so too, and so did Dawn Jackson of The Lance, another Winnipeg community paper. Glen titled his article on the Faith Page, "**Man has Mission, Vision**". Dawn wrote in the Lance, "Unlike Sampson, Rev. gains through a haircut".

Those who work in the media are people. Your relationship with them needs to be cultivated and maintained. You can do that most effectively by putting good stories into their hands. By providing all the essentials of a potential story they will response to future stories you may deliver to them. Such practices will open doors and provide more opportunities to turn your top stories into a headline.

As you cross paths with media personnel exchange business cards with them. Inquire about what stories they are working on. Compliment them on the articles they have already written.

CHAPTER SUMMARY

- Treat media personnel with respect.
- Provide adequate information for their research.
- Provide them with good news tips and leads.

FOUR

RECOGNIZE A NEWSWORTHY STORY

Principle Four: My father often said if you get one idea from a book it is worth the price of the book. In this chapter you will learn the price of admission. In other words these next paragraphs will be worth for more than the price of this book

There are newsworthy events happening every day. Some of them are happening right in your backyard. Learn to discern what a newsworthy story is and what media would be most likely to publish or broadcast them. To help in developing this understanding read their newspapers and listen to their news reports on the radio and television. What stories are they reporting? What type of story are they looking for? Better yet ask the media directly. Ask a reporter or editor what stories they are working on. What stories do they value the most? Suggest that maybe you could help them with some leads. This researching will increase your understanding of what stories are newsworthy.

In the winter of 2001 I was offered and and accepted the position of executive of Mission Possible. As I was preparing to make move from Winnipeg to Vancouver I faxed a news release to CBC Radio One about my pending departure. Later that day I received a call from Dameon Wall of CBC Radio inviting me down to their studio on

Portage Avenue for a live interview. During the four years I had been associated with Siloam Mission CBC Radio had done six different pieces about Siloam Mission. In comparison with similar agencies in Winnipeg we were a rather small organization with an operating budget of approximately $ 80,000. After that live interview I asked Dameon why had CBC radio shown such repeated interest in such a relatively small organization.

WHY HAD THEY SHOWN SUCH INTEREST?

Among others things he said that we were accessible. Each news release that I sent out included my name, phone numbers, fax, and email. I had kept in touch by sending numerous news releases to CBC radio. They knew how to get in touch with us. The major reason he said was that Siloam Mission was a story that just kept on going. First it was our compassionate service to the poor of our neighbourhood by David White. In that story we had told about the thirteen hundred meals we had served to the needy people in our neighbourhood each year. Then it was the major story about our ongoing negotiations with the City of Winnipeg. Then it was the story I broke to them about the settlement with the city. I had broken that agreement to them first. That was followed by our year of searching for a new location. Then it was the grand reopening at our new location at 564 Main Street. Finally, it was my departure as executive director going to Mission Possible in Vancouver.

I remember that conversation because of what he said next. He described to me what is the defining characteristic of a newsworthy story. He told me that change is the key factor of making a story newsworthy. Whenever there is change that is the factor that increases the media's interest. He defined change is something new, something old. It is a beginning. It is an ending. It is the beginning of a new program or the end of an old program. It is the hiring of new staff. It is the departure of staff. It is change of location. It is change of policy. These are characteristics of potential newsworthy stories. These are the factors which trigger stories into breaking news.

Looking back at my experience at Siloam Mission there were a number of significant changes that kept attracting the media. In a period of 48 months we experienced numerous changes. So I should not have been surprised when on October 17, 2000 we had we had the grand opening at our new location there was a positive response from the media, especially television. I had invited three special guests for that occasion; The Right Honourable George Hicks, speaker of the Manitoba Legislature, Lillian Thomas, the Deputy Mayor of Winnipeg, and Rev. Lorne Meisner, the President of the Evangelical Fellowship of Manitoba. As was our practice we sent out news releases announcing this significant ribbon cutting ceremony. All four local television stations in Winnipeg responded by sending a reporter along with a camera crew. In addition there were two newspapers reporters. That evening at the six o'clock news spot on these four channels there was a story about Siloam Mission's grand reopening. While CBC TV gave us only ten seconds, CKY-TV featured the opening for two minutes. That was public exposure that we could not have afforded to purchase. They all recognized that this was a time to celebrate. To the city's media this was a newsworthy story because it was about change. It was a new start.

Remember that the most appealing component in a news story is change. The question to be asked is what is happening in your organization that has an element of change in it? Learn to spin those changes into top news stories. When you do

CHANGE IS THE KEY

something new or different you are positioning your story to make headlines.

One of the better headlines I have ever made was on the first Christmas dinner after I had assumed the position of executive director of Siloam Mission, We did something that had never been done before. I decided that the people we served in the inner city deserved the opportunity to help others. I wanted to create a feel good situation. So we invited all our guests to our first annual Christmas dinner to make a donation toward the relief work that was taking place in North Korea. This funding campaign was being sponsored by the Canadian Foodgrains Bank located in Winnipeg. I had contacted in advance Trish Jordan of CFGB who supplied us with plenty of materials to promote this project. The response was so rewarding. The 180 guests that cold Manitoba winter night gave $ 76.00. That may not seem much to you and me but it was to our guests. One envelop that our treasure Eric Tapley opened that night contained just a single dime. Most people followed our suggestion and gave a dollar. One of our volunteers gave $ 100. When the CIDA matched those donations we had raised an amazing total of $ 1,200.

As we were planning this event I thought this had the potential of making a top headline. So I faxed a news release to the local media. Nancy Westaway from the Winnipeg Free Press called me at home for an interview. Then that evening she sent a photographer for the Christmas Dinner. I told her I could fax the results of the collection if she was interested. She indicated that yes she was. So I then thought for sure they would print this story the following morning.

The big surprise came early the next morning when I retrieved the paper from our front porch. I remember going out on that cold porch in stocking feet. I took the paper into our kitchen, sat down and poured myself a cup of coffee. Then I quickly scanned the paper looking for that story and a possible picture. I could not find anything. I leafed through the pages a couple of times because I was sure our story would be printed. With great disappointment I folded up the paper on the kitchen table and poured myself another cup of coffee. With that sadness and my head hanging low I happen to look at the front page and saw it! Our story had not only made the headlines it was the top story. It read, *"Poor Gladly Give What they Can"* There we were on the front page with the lead story for the province's largest paper. There was Russell Sinclair one of our guests in a coloured picture. Underneath the picture was the line, *"Russell Sinclair saying he feels good about making a contribution to North Korean famine relief."*

IT WAS THE HEADLINER

Who benefited from that story? Obviously Siloam Mission did. The people of the inner city did because they were put in a better light as they were portrayed as they really were people with a heart. So did the Canadian Foodgrains Bank, and the thirteen denominations who work with CFGB in providing relief throughout the world. If getting the media's attention is key to marketing a non-profit organization we had achieved it. We had done it and it had not cost us a dollar. Just some imagination, some invitations and a faxed news release.

An editor had made a decision that put our story on their front page the Sunday before Christmas. It would not have happened if we had kept the good things we were doing to ourselves. I believe that this story made the valued service we were providing more visible. It said to our core of volunteers that what we were doing together was of significant value. It put Siloam Mission on the map!

WHAT WE WERE DOING
TOGETHER WAS OF VALUE

And now the rest of the story. A couple of days after this story appeared in the Free Press a Korean lady called me on the phone. She first wanted to validate this story. She asked, "Did these people in the inner city actually give $75.00 for the famine in North Korea?" I said yes they had certainly done what the newspaper had reported. She was overwhelmed that some street people in the core area of our city cared enough about her people living on the other side of the world. She told me she would match what they gave. A couple of days later I received in the mail a cheque for $ 75.00. Can you imagine how good our guests felt when I told them about that phone call and the Korean lady's cheque? As Russell Sinclair had said to the reporter that night it felt good making a contribution to the North Korean famine relief. Now we all felt good, the 180 guests, and the twenty volunteers that served a full course Christmas turkey dinner one cold Winnipeg December night.

BE READY TO BE BUMPED

The next year in 1998 we repeated the same event at our Annual Christmas Dinner. That evening the temperature was minus -35c with the wind chill factored in. We had distributed 180 tickets, but only 140 had attended. All the money donated that evening was given for the CFGB relief work for those affected by Hurricane Mitch in Central America. Again we sent out a news release outlining what we were going to do. Again I was interviewed by phone. This time the reporter was Alexandra Paul who was also from the Winnipeg Free Press. The newsworthy item this year in addition to the fundraising for Central America was that the Deputy Mayor of Winnipeg, Lillian Thomas was coming with her son David to help serve. The Free Press sent one of their staff photographers Joe Bryksa to capture the event on film. We made the paper again, but this time the story made only page six. The reason was there was the possibility that US President Bill Clinton would be impeached in Washington, DC. A bigger newsworthy story had bumped our story. Despite that the article gave me another opportunity to express our appreciation to those who had helped make the supper possible and our principle funding partner, the Church of the Nazarene in western Canada.

WHY WOULD TEENS SPEND THEIR SUMMER AT AN INNER CITY MISSION?

I have found it simply amazing how repeatedly the various media platforms have responded to the stories I have sent to them. Another example is in the summer of 1997 when a group of ten teens and led by their youth leaders Steve and Linda Alcorn came from the First Church of the Nazarene in Red Deer, Alberta. They came to help with some light construction work at Siloam Mission. They paid their way. They also paid for the supplies we used and they spent seven days of their summer holidays. As was my practice I sent out a number of new releases to the media. Among them was the local CTV affiliate CKY-TV. They reported this youth group's trip to Winnipeg's inner city. The question I raised in my release was why teens would spend their summer at an inner city mission. In addition to this exposure a local Christian program on Trinity Television's *It's a New Day* sent a reporter who featured this story in one of their daily Kingdom Reports. I also faxed a news release back to the Red Deer Advocate which sparked some additional coverage when that team returned home.

George Barnaby was a volunteer at Siloam Mission when I became executive director of Siloam Mission. George lived in the Bell Hotel, one of those rundown places where street people often resided. We almost immediately connected. It soon became our practice that every Wednesday morning we would meet and look for a new place to have coffee. At first I wanted to have an understanding of what it was like to live on social assistance and see the adjacent neighbourhood through his eyes.

In the spring of 1999 I decided to volunteer some of my time for the upcoming Winnipeg Pan American Games scheduled for that summer. I suggested to George that he do that same. When he signed up as a volunteer they gave him as they did every volunteer a Pan Am uniform. Included in that package was a volunteer lapel pin. George became so fascinated with this pin that he began collecting and exchanging for other pins. Any kind of pin, any shape and from anywhere. His enthusiasm about this new found hobby went over the top. So I offered to help George collect more pins. Here was the deal that I made with him. If he would do the research and find the fax numbers of municipalities in Canada I would fax a request on his behalf to these different Canadian cities and towns. It was not long before he had collected one hundred. That was a story for perhaps a local community newspaper. So I made arrangements with his

MLA, The Honourable George Hicks to present his special pin as speaker of the Manitoba Legislature. Valorie Church reported this presentation in The Times community newspaper with a picture of the three of us, the two Georges and me.

THE PINS JUST
KEPT ON COMING

The story however did not die with this presentation because George just kept on collecting pins. Week after week the pins just kept on coming to our mail box. I was amazed to discover that even the smallest towns and villages in Canada had their own collectors pin. When he reached the 500 level with the help of my friend Douglas Martindale MLA we arranged to have the Right Honourable Peter Liba, the Lieutenant Governor of Manitoba present George a special pin. In addition to Valorie Church covering this continuing story much to my surprise a camera crew from Winnipeg's CKY-TV arrived just in time for this presentation.

The perks of this occasion was having the Lieutenant Governor present me also with his special lapel pin. Also The Times report included some information about Siloam Mission. George, who became known is affectionately as "Pinhead", kept on collecting lapel pins. This story clued me into another factor in getting a story into print. If you can include an important name in the news release, because names of VIPs make good headlines.

Right Honourable Peter Liba, Lieutenant Governor of Manitoba, presents George Barmby with his 500th pin, with Rev. Doug Woods looking on.

Pin collector nets 500th souvenir

By Valorie J. Church
Times Correspondent

At last count Winnipeg's "Pin" ambassador, the now-famous Pan Am Games volunteer George Barmby, had reached a total of 145 pins.

That was in March.

On Aug. 28 he was presented with his 500th pin by the Right Honourable

Peter Liba, Lieutenant Governor of Manitoba.

Barmby had never considered the hobby prior to the 1999 games. It was something that was borne out of the thrill and pride it gave him to wear his Pan Am volunteer pin that encouraged him to continue his pursuit following the games.

"Every volunteer received a uniform," he said. "It came with a pin and that's how it all started."

Liba presented him with a pin of the Lieutenant Governor's standard, an exact replica of the flag that flies over government house. "I hope this leads to 1,000 pins or even more," he said. "On this occasion I would also like to present you with a Manitoba Millenium Medal which we had printed specially this year to present to citizens like yourself."

Continued on page 12

When I suggested to my wife Dawn and her business partner Evangeline Keeley that we do a news release on their custom sewing business we had no prominent name to attach to the story. I thought however that we had a story with a different twist, something a little different. The angle I took was that Evangeline was a professional musician whose hobby was sewing. That was a story.

SHE SAW A LITTLE DIFFERENT STORY

Dawn Clarke, the editor of the Lance community newspaper responded to the news release. She saw a little different story when she interviewed the two ladies. She had them pose with their sewing machines. The article's headline read, *"Hobby turns into business*". Here were two friends who had turned a hobby into a cottage industry. Both of them had always done a lot of sewing for themselves. So they launched a small craft business that specialized in baby items they called *Peace Work*.

Hobby turns into business

By Dawn Clarke
Lance Editor

A hobby has turned into a cottage industry for Evangeline Keeley and Dawn Woods.

Five years ago, the friends decided to take their sewing public by starting a small business known as Peace Work.

Now they take their creations, from baby accessories to adult sweatshirts, to craft sales around the city.

"We were doing a lot of sewing for ourselves and for people we knew when it occurred to us that we might be able to make a go of it," said Woods, who lives in East Kildonan.

"We started making placemats and bibs and little jogging suits for babies, and it just evolved from there."

Unique creations

Keeley, a Fort Garry resident, says the duo works with all sorts of patterns and materials to create one-of-a-kind quality items.

"That's why I sew for myself. Partly it's for economic reasons, but I also like the fact that I won't be wearing the same clothes as everyone else," said Keeley, a professional musician.

The business partners say they can also customize their creations, such as handmade sweaters or

Evangeline Keeley (left) and Dawn Woods sew up a storm for their business, Peace Work.

Peace Work will be at Grant Park Shopping Centre until Nov. 13 as part of the Red River Art and Craft Show.

Then from Nov. 18-Dec. 24, their work will be for sale at a store rented by the Guild of Manitoba Artisans

in Fort Richmond Plaza 2860 Pembina Hwy.

Items by Peace Work are also on sale at Cherished Creations and Academy General Store.

For more information please call Evangeline (269-7549) or Dawn (663-3717).

I have found that these principles for telling your story work not only for non-profit organizations and churches, but for individuals. The lead pastor of the church that Dawn and I are a part of urges us to practice hospitality. For over ten years we have had as our Christmas guests homeless people from Vancouver's Downtown Eastside. During the weeks leading up to the 2010 Advent season we decided that we would expand this practice of hospitality. Since Dawn teaches an ESL class at the First Church of the Nazarene in Vancouver, BC and I lead a small group in the Alpha program which consisted of some of her ESL students we invited this group of recent immigrants to Canada as our guests for Christmas dinner. About a dozen indicated that they were coming. They were from Sri Lanka, mainland China and Mexico City. A day before we hosted our Christmas dinner I emailed a news release to two local community papers and two Vancouver TV stations. Within five minutes one TV station phoned and indicated their interest. Later another station called asking if it would be OK for them to come.

On Christmas Day a crew from the local Global TV station arrived at our celebration. The cameraman stayed and filmed the entire event. Later that evening our new friends gathered around our TV and watched ourselves on the BC TV Global news at 6:00 pm. A week later a local reporter's article appeared in one of Richmond's community paper entitled "No Strangers at this Table." Alan Campbell pointed out personal practice of inviting new immigrants into our how to celebrate the Christmas holiday. That was so heartwarming to have about a dozen guests from Sri Lanka, Russia and Mexico City.

CHAPTER SUMMARY

- Change is the major characteristic of a newsworthy story.
- How do you spell change in your story?
- A Good story may be bumped by a better one.
- Are you doing something different?

A NOTE TO MY READERS

An optimist is the man who reaches for his hat when the preacher says, "In conclusion". Here is my conclusion, my summary of what I have been saying. The most effective means of communicating is through the media. Having your story retold through a newspaper headline or broadcast on television carries far more weight than any other form of communication. By getting your story into the main stream of modern media you will inspire unknown support in terms of volunteers, additional financial resources and public good will. You may think as I once did that getting your story into main stream media is beyond the realm of possibility. The stories that I have written illustrate the truth that your stories too can be turned into headlines. Follow the simply principles that I have outlined and make them routine practices and you will be surprised as I have at the result. I stumbled across these foundational practices accidentally. Now that you have these truths laid out before you and your organization go and turn your stories into headline. It's time to start thinking headlines!

WHEN BAD NEWS COMES KNOCKING

Crisis management: I have been involved in at least one situation when I did not have good news to report but bad news. On that occasion the media came knocking with a camera crew. The bad news was that a former staff member had a moral failure and subsequently had been arrested. If you are ever involved in such an event here are the steps that I would recommend that you need to take. My first advice is tell the truth. Don't attempt to spin the issue. Keep your integrity and the integrity of the organization that you are representing. Secondly if members of the media are attempting to interview don't be evasive and try to hide from them. |On that particular occasion when things went south one of my staff members attempted to chase the media away. It was a TV crew from a local station which was an affiliate of a national TV network. When I heard of this I immediately got the reporters phone number and called her. I invited her and the camera crew to my office.

You don't have to answer all the questions that are posed by the media, but be as transparent as possible. In this particular incident the media wanted a picture of the individual who was the centre of the story. I told them I didn't have a picture, which I didn't. I added if I did I would not release it to them. Prepare in advance for various scenarios. Again let me say if you have time prepare in advance. Preparation is of strategic importance. In the time available try to imagine why the media would be interested in the story. Talk it over. If possible prepare in advance a news release that has the correct contact information including addresses. In that NR name the issue and explain it. Put heads together in advance and think about possible questions that the media may ask. Make someone available to deal with the press. Prepare people in advance with information they should know and advise them when approached by the media to direct all question to the one principle spokesperson. This individual should be well prepared. It will sit well with the press if a no comment is made by a representative coupled with redirection to a spokesperson with adequate contact information who has access to a news release. Stay focused on one theme that is outlined in your news release. Narrow your response down to one or two items. If it is necessary to postpone your response to any inquires and you need to tell the media you will get back to them. Then keep your promise.

That will establish your integrity. Don't be afraid of the media. After the incident is passed do some follow-up. Give the people who reported the story a call and thank them for their reporting. This will be a significant step in building future relationship. This will help cultivate your relationship with the media.

In the incident in which I was the primary spokesperson I happen to recognized the cameraman. He had done some positive reporting on a previous occasion with me. So I thanked him and the reporter with him for taking the time to cover the incident even though it was far from good news.

NOTES AND NEWS RELEASES

Well written news releases are key to turning your story into a headline. It is a skill that comes with careful thought and repeated practice. Since newspapers and other media outlets receive hundreds of news releases every day you can assured that most received only a cursory glance. If your first sentence does not get the news editor's attention it will unlikely become that day's headline. It is very unlikely that the editor will read the first paragraph or even scan your entire news release. Here are some example news releases that did catch the news editor's eye.

NEWS RELEASE

Release Date: December 17, 1997

Contact Person:
Douglas C. Woods,
Executive Director Siloam Mission
707 Main St. Winnipeg, MB
(204) 663-3717 H/O, Fax 669-8119

INNER CITY CARES FOR OTHERS

Siloam Mission is providing those of the inner city the opportunity to care for others. Those who frequent the inner city mission for warm clothing, nutritious food and spiritual support have been made aware of the severity of the current famine in North Korea. This Saturday evening December 20th. at the Mission's Annual Christmas Dinner those who attend will be challenge to contribute according to their means to those suffering from the North Korean famine. Executive Director Douglas Woods believes that even those on the Main Street strip should be given the opportunity to help others in their time of need. The annual Christmas dinner as usual is open anyone without cost, but donations will be received which will then be turned over to the Canadian Foodgrains Bank for the shipment of grain to this nation of twenty-two million people who are in the grip of their national food crisis.

NEWS RELEASE

Date: December 19, 1998

Contact Person: Rev. Douglas Woods

Phone: 956-4344 or 663-3717 (H)

DEPUTY MAYOR OFFERS TO SERVE AT MISSION

Deputy Mayor Lillian Thomas of Winnipeg will be helping to serve at Siloam Mission's Christmas Supper tonight. Along side with local businessmen, board members of the Mission, pastors, and regular volunteers Lillian Thomas will be assisting in serving over 180 special guests at the Siloam Mission Annual Christmas Supper.

At each of the three sittings beginning at 5:00 p.m. through to 9:00 p.m. the guests will be served a traditional turkey dinner with all the trimmings including pumpkin pie. There will be gifts for everyone and special door prizes. The rumour is that even Santa Claus himself will make a special appearance.

This Christmas event has been made possible through the generous donations of business, churches, interested individuals, Penner IGA and Winnipeg Harvest. The guests will be given the opportunity to make a donation to the Mitch Hurricane Relief through the

CPSIA information can be obtained
at www.ICGtesting.com
Printed in the USA
BVHW031529110921
616361BV00002B/123